PIANO • VOCAL • GUITAR

GOODBYE SONGS

ISBN 978-1-5400-9425-4

Visit Hal Leonard Online at
www.halleonard.com

Contact Us:
Hal Leonard
7777 West Bluemound Road
Milwaukee, WI 53213
Email: info@halleonard.com

In Europe, contact:
Hal Leonard Europe Limited
42 Wigmore Street
Marylebone, London, W1U 2RN
Email: info@halleonardeurope.com

In Australia, contact:
Hal Leonard Australia Pty. Ltd.
4 Lentara Court
Cheltenham, Victoria, 3192 Australia
Email: info@halleonard.com.au

BEFORE YOU GO

Words and Music by LEWIS CAPALDI,
BENJAMIN KOHN, PETER KELLEHER,
THOMAS BARNES and PHILIP PLESTED

Moderately fast

I fell by the way-side, ___ like ev-'ry-one else.
Was nev-er the right time ___ when-ev-er you called.

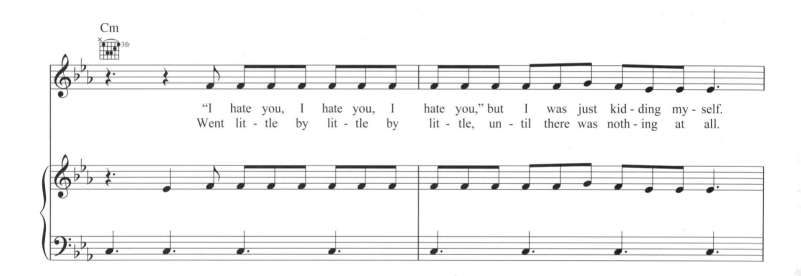

"I hate you, I hate you, I hate you," but I was just kid-ding my-self.
Went lit-tle by lit-tle by lit-tle, un-til there was noth-ing at all.

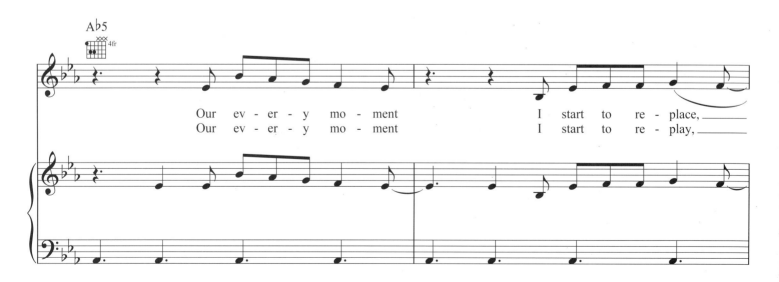

Our ev-er-y mo-ment I start to re-place, ___
Our ev-er-y mo-ment I start to re-play, ___

CANDLE IN THE WIND

Words and Music by ELTON JOHN
and BERNIE TAUPIN

Good-bye, Nor-ma Jean, _____ though I nev-er _____ knew you _____ at all
Lone-li-ness _____ was tough, _____ the tough-est role _____ you ev-er played.

you had the grace to hold your-self _____ while those a-round _____ you crawled.
Hol-ly-wood cre-at-ed a su-per-star _____ and pain was the price you paid. _____

They crawled out of the wood-work
E-ven when you died,

12

THE HARDEST THING

Words and Music by STEVE KIPNER
and DAVID FRANK

FAREWELL

Words and Music by ESTHER DEAN
and ALEXANDER GRANT

Moderate Ballad

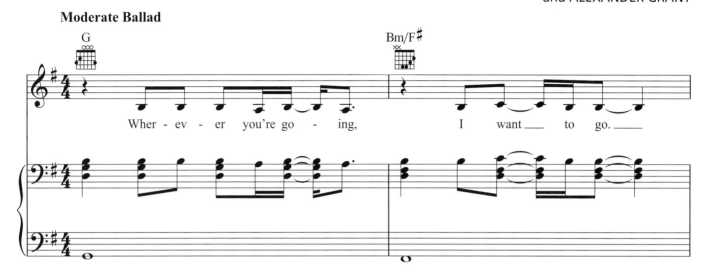

Wher- ev- er you're go - ing, I want ___ to go. ___

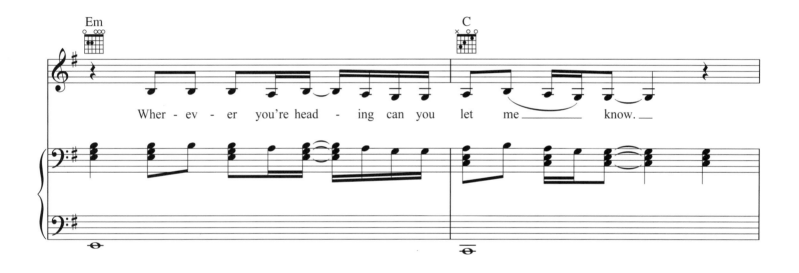

Wher- ev- er you're head - ing can you let me ___ know. ___

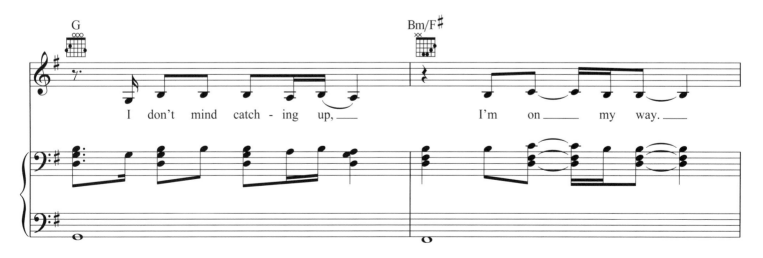

I don't mind catch- ing up, ___ I'm on ___ my way. ___

50 WAYS TO SAY GOODBYE

Words and Music by PAT MONAHAN,
ESPEN LIND and AMUND BJØRKLUND

* *Recorded a half step lower.*

I wan-na live a thou-sand lives ___ with you. ___ I wan-

FRIENDS

Words and Music by MICHAEL W. SMITH
and DEBORAH D. SMITH

Packing up the dreams God plant - ed
With the faith and love God's giv - en

in the fer - tile soil of you,
spring - ing from the hope we know,

life - time's not ____ too long _____ to live ____ as friends. __

And __ friends are friends __ for - ev - er if the

Lord's the Lord __ of them, __ and a friend will not __ say "nev - er" 'cause the

GOODBYE

Words and Music by
ALICIA KEYS

* Vocals written one octave above recorded pitch.

D.S. al Coda

man that he is.

CODA

(find the words to say Is this the good - bye)?

end? Are you sure?
(End?) (Are you sure?)

How should you know when you've nev - er been here be -
(Nev - er been

GOODBYE TO LOVE

Words and Music by RICHARD CARPENTER
and JOHN BETTIS

Repeat ad lib. and Fade

HAPPIER

Words and Music by MARSHMELLO,
STEVE MAC and DAN SMITH

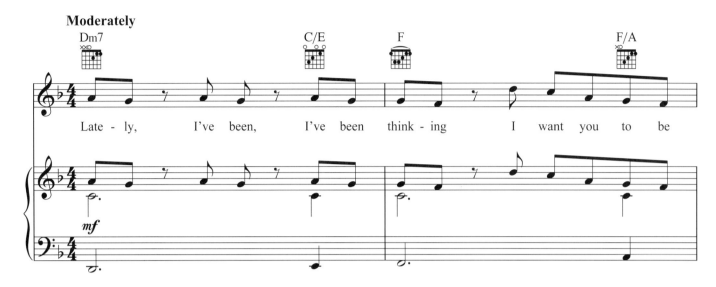

Late - ly, I've been, I've been think - ing I want you to be

hap - pi - er, I want you to be hap - pi - er. _____ When the morn - ing

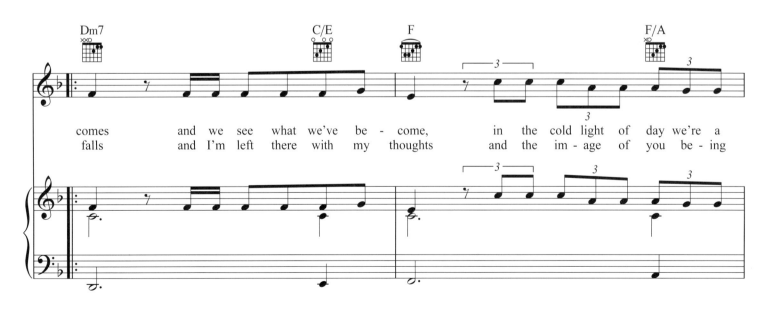

comes and we see what we've be - come, in the cold light of day we're a

falls and I'm left there with my thoughts and the im - age of you be - ing

HERE COMES GOODBYE

Words and Music by CHRIS SLIGH
and CLINT LAGERBERG

Moderately, in 2

I can hear the truck ___ tires com- in' up ___ the grav- el ___ road, ___ and it's not ___

Here comes good - bye.

dim.

mp

I WILL REMEMBER YOU
Theme from THE BROTHERS McMULLEN

Words and Music by SARAH McLACHLAN,
SEAMUS EGAN and DAVE MERENDA

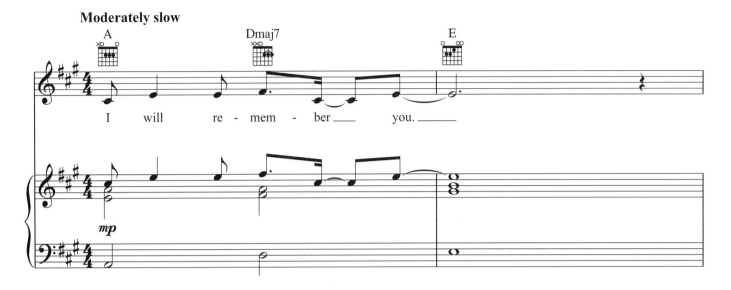

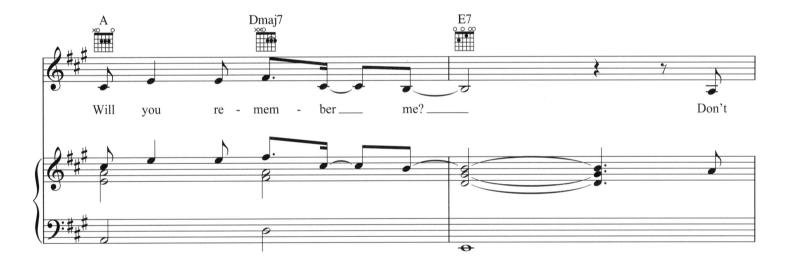

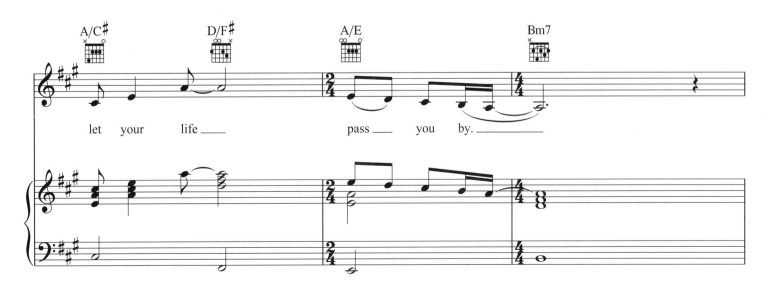

HOW CAN I HELP YOU SAY GOODBYE

Words and Music by BURTON COLLINS
and KAREN TAYLOR-GOOD

Through the back __ win-dow of our fif-ty-nine __ wa-gon I

Sit-tin' with __ Ma-ma a-lone in her __ bed-room,

watched my best __ friend Ja-mie slip-pin' fur-ther a-way. _____

she o-pened her __ eyes __ and then squeezed my hand. _____ She said,

IT'S SO HARD TO SAY GOODBYE TO YESTERDAY

Words and Music by FREDDIE PERREN
and CHRISTINE YARIAN

How do I _____ say good-bye _____ to what __ we had? _____
know _____ where this road _____ is going to lead. _____

_____ The good times _____ that made us laugh _____ out-weighed the
_____ All I know _____ is where we've been _____ and what we've

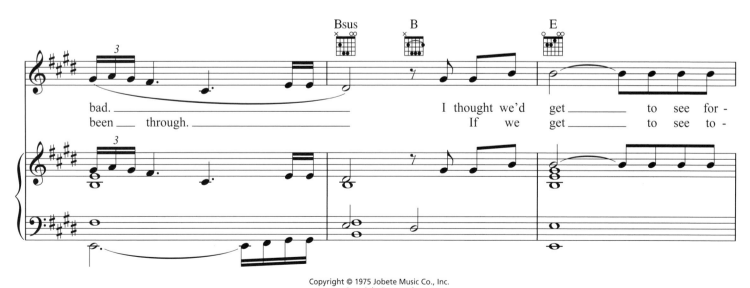

bad. _____ I thought we'd get _____ to see for-
been __ through. _____ If we get _____ to see to-

LEAVING ON A JET PLANE

Words and Music by
JOHN DENVER

'Cause I'm leav - in' on a jet ___ plane;

don't know when I'll be back ___ a - gain. Oh babe, I hate ___ to ___

go. _____ { There's so go. _____ 'Cause I'm

Repeat and Fade

leav - in' }
Leav - in' } on a jet ___ plane; don't know when I'll be back ___ a - gain.

MONSTERS

Words and Music by JAMES BLUNT,
AMY WADGE and JIMMY HOGARTH

SAY SOMETHING

Words and Music by IAN AXEL,
CHAD VACCARINO and MIKE CAMPBELL

NEITHER ONE OF US
(Wants to Be the First to Say Goodbye)

Words and Music by
JIM WEATHERLY

NEVER SAY GOODBYE

Words and Music by JON BON JOVI
and RICHIE SAMBORA

say good-bye, ___ nev-er say good-bye, ___

hold-in' on, ___ we got to try, ___ hold-in' on ___ to nev-er say good-bye. ___

NO GOOD IN GOODBYE

Words and Music by MARK SHEEHAN,
DANIEL O'DONOGHUE and JAMES BARRY

Moderate Rock

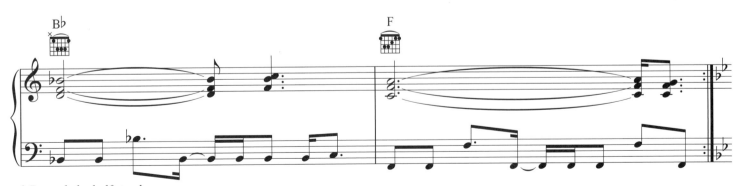

* Recorded a half step lower.

SEE YOU AGAIN

from FURIOUS 7

Words and Music by CAMERON THOMAZ,
CHARLIE PUTH, JUSTIN FRANKS,
ANDREW CEDAR, DANN HUME,
JOSH HARDY and PHOEBE COCKBURN

TEARS IN HEAVEN

featured in the Motion Picture RUSH

Words and Music by ERIC CLAPTON
and WILL JENNINGS

Be - yond the door _____ there's peace, I'm sure, _

SOMEONE LIKE YOU

Words and Music by ADELE ADKINS
and DAN WILSON

could-n't stay a - way, _ I could-n't fight it. I had hoped you'd see my face and that you'd be re-mind-ed that, for

me, _____ it is-n't o - ver. _____

D.S. al Coda

CODA

lasts in love, but some-times it hurts in - stead." _____

Noth-ing com - pares, no wor - ries or cares, re - grets and mis - takes, they're mem - o - ries made.

SUPERMARKET FLOWERS

Words and Music by ED SHEERAN,
BENJAMIN LEVIN and JOHNNY McDAID

Moderately, with feeling

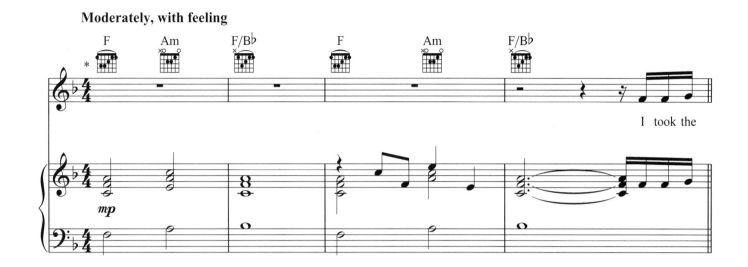

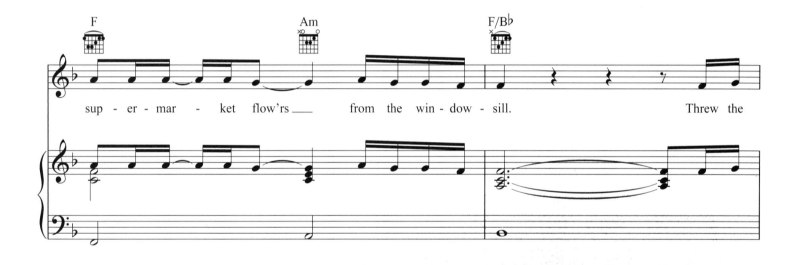

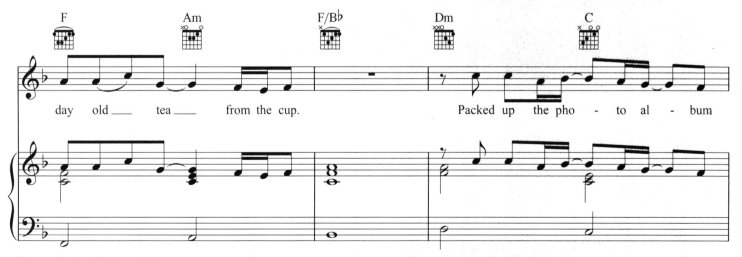

* Recorded a half step higher.

TIME TO SAY GOODBYE
(Con te partirò)

Words by LUCIO QUARANTOTTO
and FRANK PETERSON
Music by FRANCESCO SARTORI

Verse 1:

Quan-do so-no so-lo so-gno al-l'o-riz-zon-te e man-can le pa-ro-le,

si lo so che non c'è lu-ce in u-na stan-za quan-do man-ca il so-le, se non ci sei

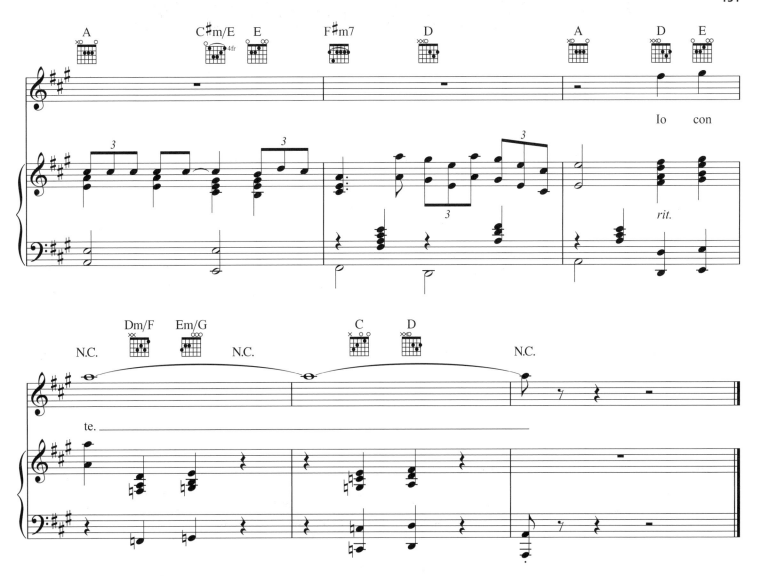

English literal translation:
Verse 1:
When I'm alone, I dream of the horizon and words fail me.
There is no light in a room where there is no sun.
And there is no sun if you're not here with me, with me.
From every window, unfurl my heart, the heart that you have won.
Into me you've poured the light, the light that you've found by the side of the road.

Chorus:
Time to say goodbye. Places that I've never seen or experienced with you,
Now I shall. I'll sail with you upon ships across the seas,
Seas that exist no more. It's time to say goodbye.

Verse 2:
When you're far away, I dream of the horizon and words fail me.
And, of course, I know that you're with me, with me.
You, my moon, you are with me.
My sun, you're here with me, with me, with me, with me.

Chorus:
Time to say goodbye. Places that I've never seen or experienced with you,
Now I shall. I'll sail with you upon ships across the seas,
Seas that exist no more, I'll revive them with you.

Tag:
I'll go with you upon ships across the seas,
Seas that exist no more, I'll revive them with you.
I'll go with you, I'll go with you.

TOO GOOD AT GOODBYES

Words and Music by SAM SMITH,
TOR HERMANSEN, MIKKEL ERIKSEN
and JAMES NAPIER

Pop Ballad

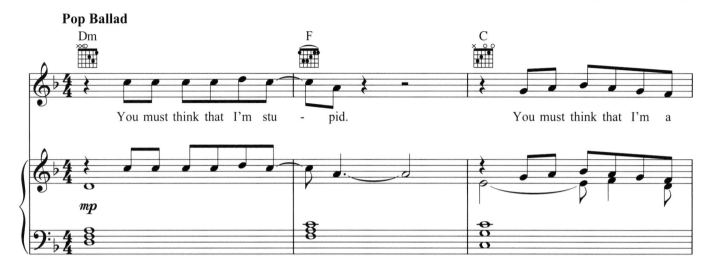

You must think that I'm stu-pid. You must think that I'm a

fool. You must think that I'm new ___ to this, ___ but I have seen this all be-fore. I'm

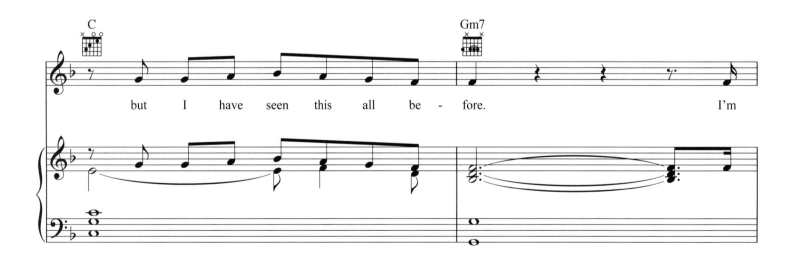